# Baby Names

*The ultimate baby names guide for boys and girls, including popular names, famous names, unique names, and more!*

# Table of Contents

# Introduction

Thank you for taking the time to pick up this book of the best baby names!

Included in this book is an enormous range of different baby names! Picking a name for your new son or daughter is meant to be a fun and exciting time, but unfortunately for many it can be quite stressful.

This book aims to solve that problem by helping you to make the right choice, whilst making the process, fun, easy, and enjoyable!

Congratulations on your baby news! Thanks for choosing this book to help you to decide on the perfect name for your new bundle of joy. I hope you find it to be helpful, and wish you the very best of luck!

# Chapter 1:
# Choosing The Right Name

Choosing the right name for your new child can be a stressful task, but it can also be very fun and exciting!

Before you begin to go through the names in this book, remember that this is meant to be an enjoyable and exciting experience. So, keep it light, put your feet up, and remember to enjoy the process!

You may want to choose a unique name for your child, a popular name, a famous name, or perhaps the same name of someone who's been instrumental in your life. Whatever you choose, keep in mind that you want your child to be proud of their title throughout their life.

I recommend going through this book and at first simply making note of the names you like the most. Pick 5 or 10 potential candidates. You may want to do this with your partner, or do it separately and then compare lists afterwards.

Whatever names you both life/dislike, remember that it's about your child – and not all about you. Pick a name that your child will love and be proud to bear. Also, picking a name that goes well with the child's surname is always a great thing to make sure of.

If you can't decide on just one name, you can always pick 1 or more middle names for your child.

Most of all, remember to take a relaxed approach to this. It's a fun and exciting time in your life, so enjoy yourself. Once again, congratulations, and good luck!

# Chapter 2:
# The Most Popular Boy's Names

Congratulations, it's a boy!

This chapter contains a list of the 1000 most popular names for boys.

1. Jacob
2. Ethan
3. Michael
4. Jayden
5. William
6. Alexander
7. Noah
8. Daniel
9. Aiden
10. Anthony
11. Joshua
12. Mason
13. Christopher
14. Andrew
15. David
16. Matthew
17. Logan
18. Elijah
19. James
20. Joseph
21. Gabriel

22. Benjamin
23. Ryan
24. Samuel
25. Jackson
26. John
27. Nathan
28. Jonathan
29. Christian
30. Liam
31. Dylan
32. Landon
33. Caleb
34. Tyler
35. Lucas
36. Evan
37. Gavin
38. Nicholas
39. Isaac
40. Brayden
41. Luke
42. Angel
43. Brandon
44. Jack
45. Isaiah
46. Jordan
47. Owen
48. Carter

49. Connor
50. Justin
51. Jose
52. Jeremiah
53. Julian
54. Robert
55. Aaron
56. Adrian
57. Wyatt
58. Kevin
59. Hunter
60. Cameron
61. Zachary
62. Thomas
63. Charles
64. Austin
65. Eli
66. Chase
67. Henry
68. Sebastian
69. Jason
70. Levi
71. Xavier
72. Ian
73. Colton
74. Dominic
75. Juan

76. Cooper
77. Josiah
78. Luis
79. Ayden
80. Carson
81. Adam
82. Nathaniel
83. Brody
84. Tristan
85. Diego
86. Parker
87. Blake
88. Oliver
89. Cole
90. Carlos
91. Jaden
92. Jesus
93. Alex
94. Aidan
95. Eric
96. Hayden
97. Bryan
98. Max
99. Jaxon
100. Brian
101. Bentley
102. Alejandro

103. Sean
104. Nolan
105. Riley
106. Kaden
107. Kyle
108. Micah
109. Vincent
110. Antonio
111. Colin
112. Bryce
113. Miguel
114. Giovanni
115. Timothy
116. Jake
117. Kaleb
118. Steven
119. Caden
120. Bryson
121. Damian
122. Grayson
123. Kayden
124. Jesse
125. Brady
126. Ashton
127. Richard
128. Victor
129. Patrick

130. Marcus
131. Preston
132. Joel
133. Santiago
134. Maxwell
135. Ryder
136. Edward
137. Miles
138. Hudson
139. Asher
140. Devin
141. Elias
142. Jeremy
143. Ivan
144. Jonah
145. Easton
146. Jace
147. Oscar
148. Collin
149. Peyton
150. Leonardo
151. Cayden
152. Gage
153. Eduardo
154. Emmanuel
155. Grant
156. Alan

157. Conner
158. Cody
159. Wesley
160. Kenneth
161. Mark
162. Nicolas
163. Malachi
164. George
165. Seth
166. Kaiden
167. Trevor
168. Jorge
169. Derek
170. Jude
171. Braxton
172. Jaxson
173. Sawyer
174. Jaiden
175. Omar
176. Tanner
177. Travis
178. Paul
179. Camden
180. Maddox
181. Andres
182. Cristian
183. Rylan

184. Josue
185. Roman
186. Bradley
187. Axel
188. Fernando
189. Garrett
190. Javier
191. Damien
192. Peter
193. Leo
194. Abraham
195. Ricardo
196. Francisco
197. Lincoln
198. Erick
199. Drake
200. Shane
201. Cesar
202. Stephen
203. Jaylen
204. Tucker
205. Kai
206. Landen
207. Braden
208. Mario
209. Edwin
210. Avery

211. Manuel
212. Trenton
213. Ezekiel
214. Kingston
215. Calvin
216. Edgar
217. Johnathan
218. Donovan
219. Alexis
220. Israel
221. Mateo
222. Silas
223. Jeffrey
224. Weston
225. Raymond
226. Hector
227. Spencer
228. Andre
229. Brendan
230. Zion
231. Griffin
232. Lukas
233. Maximus
234. Harrison
235. Andy
236. Braylon
237. Tyson

238. Shawn

239. Sergio

240. Zane

241. Emiliano

242. Jared

243. Ezra

244. Charlie

245. Keegan

246. Chance

247. Drew

248. Troy

249. Greyson

250. Corbin

251. Simon

252. Clayton

253. Myles

254. Xander

255. Dante

256. Erik

257. Rafael

258. Martin

259. Dominick

260. Dalton

261. Cash

262. Skyler

263. Theodore

264. Marco

265. Caiden
266. Johnny
267. Ty
268. Gregory
269. Kyler
270. Roberto
271. Brennan
272. Luca
273. Emmett
274. Kameron
275. Declan
276. Quinn
277. Jameson
278. Amir
279. Bennett
280. Colby
281. Pedro
282. Emanuel
283. Malik
284. Graham
285. Dean
286. Jasper
287. Everett
288. Aden
289. Dawson
290. Angelo
291. Reid

292. Abel
293. Dakota
294. Zander
295. Paxton
296. Ruben
297. Judah
298. Jayce
299. Jakob
300. Finn
301. Elliot
302. Frank
303. Lane
304. Fabian
305. Dillon
306. Brock
307. Derrick
308. Emilio
309. Joaquin
310. Marcos
311. Ryker
312. Anderson
313. Grady
314. Devon
315. Elliott
316. Holden
317. Amari
318. Dallas

319. Corey
320. Danny
321. Cruz
322. Lorenzo
323. Allen
324. Trey
325. Leland
326. Armando
327. Rowan
328. Taylor
329. Cade
330. Colt
331. Felix
332. Adan
333. Jayson
334. Tristen
335. Julius
336. Raul
337. Braydon
338. Zayden
339. Julio
340. Nehemiah
341. Darius
342. Ronald
343. Louis
344. Trent
345. Keith

346. Payton

347. Enrique

348. Jax

349. Randy

350. Scott

351. Desmond

352. Gerardo

353. Jett

354. Dustin

355. Phillip

356. Beckett

357. Ali

358. Romeo

359. Kellen

360. Cohen

361. Pablo

362. Ismael

363. Jaime

364. Brycen

365. Larry

366. Kellan

367. Keaton

368. Gunner

369. Braylen

370. Brayan

371. Landyn

372. Walter

373. Jimmy
374. Marshall
375. Beau
376. Saul
377. Donald
378. Esteban
379. Karson
380. Reed
381. Phoenix
382. Brenden
383. Tony
384. Kade
385. Jamari
386. Jerry
387. Mitchell
388. Colten
389. Arthur
390. Brett
391. Dennis
392. Rocco
393. Jalen
394. Tate
395. Chris
396. Quentin
397. Titus
398. Cascy
399. Brooks

400. Izaiah
401. Mathew
402. King
403. Philip
404. Zackary
405. Darren
406. Russell
407. Gael
408. Albert
409. Braeden
410. Dane
411. Gustavo
412. Kolton
413. Cullen
414. Jay
415. Rodrigo
416. Alberto
417. Leon
418. Alec
419. Damon
420. Arturo
421. Waylon
422. Milo
423. Davis
424. Walker
425. Moises
426. Kobe

427. Curtis

428. Matteo

429. August

430. Mauricio

431. Marvin

432. Emerson

433. Maximilian

434. Reece

435. Orlando

436. River

437. Bryant

438. Issac

439. Yahir

440. Uriel

441. Hugo

442. Mohamed

443. Enzo

444. Karter

445. Lance

446. Porter

447. Maurice

448. Leonel

449. Zachariah

450. Ricky

451. Joe

452. Johan

453. Nikolas

454. Dexter
455. Jonas
456. Justice
457. Knox
458. Lawrence
459. Salvador
460. Alfredo
461. Gideon
462. Maximiliano
463. Nickolas
464. Talon
465. Byron
466. Orion
467. Solomon
468. Braiden
469. Alijah
470. Kristopher
471. Rhys
472. Gary
473. Jacoby
474. Davion
475. Jamarion
476. Pierce
477. Sam
478. Cason
479. Noel
480. Ramon

481. Kason

482. Mekhi

483. Shaun

484. Warren

485. Douglas

486. Ernesto

487. Ibrahim

488. Armani

489. Cyrus

490. Quinton

491. Isaias

492. Reese

493. Jaydon

494. Ryland

495. Terry

496. Frederick

497. Chandler

498. Jamison

499. Deandre

500. Dorian

501. Khalil

502. Ari

503. Franklin

504. Maverick

505. Amare

506. Muhammad

507. Ronan

508. London
509. Eddie
510. Moses
511. Roger
512. Aldo
513. Nasir
514. Demetrius
515. Adriel
516. Brodie
517. Kelvin
518. Morgan
519. Tobias
520. Ahmad
521. Keagan
522. Prince
523. Trace
524. Alvin
525. Giovani
526. Kendrick
527. Malcolm
528. Skylar
529. Conor
530. Camron
531. Abram
532. Jonathon
533. Bruce
534. Noe

535. Quincy

536. Rohan

537. Ahmed

538. Nathanael

539. Barrett

540. Remington

541. Kamari

542. Kristian

543. Kieran

544. Finnegan

545. Boston

546. Xzavier

547. Chad

548. Guillermo

549. Uriah

550. Archer

551. Rodney

552. Gunnar

553. Micheal

554. Ulises

555. Bobby

556. Aaden

557. Kamden

558. Roy

559. Kane

560. Kasen

561. Julien

562. Ezequiel
563. Lucian
564. Atticus
565. Javon
566. Melvin
567. Jeffery
568. Terrance
569. Nelson
570. Aarav
571. Carl
572. Malakai
573. Jadon
574. Triston
575. Harley
576. Jon
577. Kian
578. Alonzo
579. Cory
580. Marc
581. Moshe
582. Gianni
583. Kole
584. Dayton
585. Jermaine
586. Asa
587. Wilson
588. Felipe

589. Kale
590. Terrence
591. Nico
592. Dominik
593. Tommy
594. Kendall
595. Cristopher
596. Isiah
597. Finley
598. Tristin
599. Cannon
600. Mohammed
601. Wade
602. Kash
603. Marlon
604. Ariel
605. Madden
606. Rhett
607. Jase
608. Layne
609. Memphis
610. Allan
611. Jamal
612. Nash
613. Jessie
614. Joey
615. Reginald

616. Giovanny
617. Lawson
618. Zaiden
619. Ace
620. Korbin
621. Rashad
622. Will
623. Urijah
624. Billy
625. Aron
626. Brennen
627. Branden
628. Leonard
629. Rene
630. Kenny
631. Tomas
632. Willie
633. Darian
634. Kody
635. Brendon
636. Aydan
637. Alonso
638. Blaine
639. Arjun
640. Raiden
641. Layton
642. Marquis

643. Sincere
644. Terrell
645. Channing
646. Chace
647. Iker
648. Mohammad
649. Jordyn
650. Messiah
651. Omari
652. Santino
653. Sullivan
654. Brent
655. Raphael
656. Deshawn
657. Elisha
658. Harry
659. Luciano
660. Jefferson
661. Jaylin
662. Ray
663. Yandel
664. Aydin
665. Craig
666. Tristian
667. Zechariah
668. Bently
669. Francis

670. Toby
671. Tripp
672. Kylan
673. Semaj
674. Alessandro
675. Alexzander
676. Lee
677. Ronnie
678. Gerald
679. Dwayne
680. Jadiel
681. Javion
682. Markus
683. Kolby
684. Neil
685. Stanley
686. Makai
687. Davin
688. Teagan
689. Cale
690. Harper
691. Callen
692. Ben
693. Kaeden
694. Clark
695. Jamie
696. Damarion

697. Davian

698. Deacon

699. Jairo

700. Kareem

701. Damion

702. Jamir

703. Aidyn

704. Lamar

705. Duncan

706. Matias

707. Rex

708. Jaeden

709. Jasiah

710. Jorden

711. Vicente

712. Aryan

713. Case

714. Tyronc

715. Yusuf

716. Gavyn

717. Lewis

718. Rogelio

719. Zayne

720. Giancarlo

721. Osvaldo

722. Rolando

723. Camren

724. Luka

725. Rylee

726. Cedric

727. Jensen

728. Soren

729. Darwin

730. Draven

731. Maxim

732. Ellis

733. Nikolai

734. Bradyn

735. Mathias

736. Zackery

737. Zavier

738. Emery

739. Brantley

740. Rudy

741. Trevon

742. Alfonso

743. Beckham

744. Darrell

745. Harold

746. Jerome

747. Daxton

748. Royce

749. Jaylon

750. Rory

751. Rodolfo
752. Tatum
753. Bruno
754. Sterling
755. Gauge
756. Van
757. Hamza
758. Ayaan
759. Rayan
760. Zachery
761. Keenan
762. Jagger
763. Heath
764. Jovani
765. Killian
766. Dax
767. Junior
768. Misael
769. Roland
770. Ramiro
771. Vance
772. Alvaro
773. Bode
774. Conrad
775. Eugene
776. Augustus
777. Carmelo

778. Adrien
779. Kamron
780. Gilberto
781. Johnathon
782. Kolten
783. Wayne
784. Zain
785. Quintin
786. Steve
787. Tyrell
788. Niko
789. Antoine
790. Hassan
791. Jean
792. Coleman
793. Elian
794. Frankie
795. Valentin
796. Adonis
797. Jamar
798. Jaxton
799. Kymani
800. Bronson
801. Clay
802. Freddy
803. Jeramiah
804. Kayson

805. Hank
806. Abdiel
807. Efrain
808. Leandro
809. Yosef
810. Aditya
811. Ean
812. Konnor
813. Sage
814. Samir
815. Todd
816. Lyric
817. Deven
818. Derick
819. Jovanni
820. Valentino
821. Demarcus
822. Ishaan
823. Konner
824. Kyson
825. Deangelo
826. Matthias
827. Maximo
828. Sidney
829. Benson
830. Dilan
831. Gilbert

832. Kyron

833. Xavi

834. Bo

835. Sylas

836. Fisher

837. Marcel

838. Franco

839. Jaron

840. Alden

841. Agustin

842. Bentlee

843. Malaki

844. Westin

845. Cael

846. Jerimiah

847. Randall

848. Blaze

849. Branson

850. Brogan

851. Callum

852. Dominique

853. Justus

854. Krish

855. Rey

856. Marcelo

857. Ronin

858. Odin

859. Camryn
860. Jair
861. Izayah
862. Brice
863. Jabari
864. Mayson
865. Isai
866. Tyree
867. Mike
868. Samson
869. Stefan
870. Devan
871. Emmitt
872. Fletcher
873. Jaidyn
874. Remy
875. Casen
876. Houston
877. Santos
878. Seamus
879. Jedidiah
880. Major
881. Vincenzo
882. Gaige
883. Winston
884. Aedan
885. Deon

886. Jaycob
887. Kamryn
888. Quinten
889. Darnell
890. Jaxen
891. Deegan
892. Landry
893. Humberto
894. Jadyn
895. Salvatore
896. Aarush
897. Edison
898. Kadyn
899. Abdullah
900. Alfred
901. Ameer
902. Carsen
903. Jaydin
904. Lionel
905. Howard
906. Davon
907. Eden
908. Trystan
909. Zaire
910. Johann
911. Antwan
912. Bodhi

913. Jayvion

914. Marley

915. Theo

916. Bridger

917. Donte

918. Lennon

919. Irvin

920. Yael

921. Jencarlos

922. Arnav

923. Devyn

924. Ernest

925. Ignacio

926. Leighton

927. Leonidas

928. Octavio

929. Rayden

930. Hezekiah

931. Ross

932. Hayes

933. Lennox

934. Nigel

935. Vaughn

936. Anders

937. Keon

938. Dario

939. Leroy

940. Cortez
941. Darryl
942. Jakobe
943. Koen
944. Darien
945. Haiden
946. Legend
947. Tyrese
948. Zaid
949. Dangelo
950. Maxx
951. Pierre
952. Camdyn
953. Chaim
954. Damari
955. Sonny
956. Antony
957. Blaise
958. Cain
959. Pranav
960. Roderick
961. Yadiel
962. Eliot
963. Hugh
964. Broderick
965. Lathan
966. Makhi

967. Ronaldo
968. Ralph
969. Zack
970. Kael
971. Keyon
972. Kingsley
973. Talan
974. Yair
975. Demarion
976. Gibson
977. Reagan
978. Cristofer
979. Daylen
980. Jordon
981. Dashawn
982. Masen
983. Clarence
984. Dillan
985. Kadin
986. Rowen
987. Thaddeus
988. Yousef
989. Clinton
990. Sheldon
991. Slade
992. Joziah
993. Keshawn

994. Menachem

995. Bailey

996. Camilo

997. Destin

998. Jaquan

999. Jaydan

1000.Crew

# Chapter 3: The Most Popular Girl's Names

Congratulations it's a girl!

This chapter includes the 1000 most popular baby names!

1. Isabella
2. Sophia
3. Emma
4. Olivia
5. Ava
6. Emily
7. Abigail
8. Madison
9. Chloe
10. Mia
11. Addison
12. Elizabeth
13. Ella
14. Natalie
15. Samantha
16. Alexis
17. Lily
18. Grace
19. Hailey
20. Alyssa
21. Lillian

22. Hannah
23. Avery
24. Leah
25. Nevaeh
26. Sofia
27. Ashley
28. Anna
29. Brianna
30. Sarah
31. Zoe
32. Victoria
33. Gabriella
34. Brooklyn
35. Kaylee
36. Taylor
37. Layla
38. Allison
39. Evelyn
40. Riley
41. Amelia
42. Khloe
43. Makayla
44. Aubrey
45. Charlotte
46. Savannah
47. Zoey
48. Bella

49. Kayla
50. Alexa
51. Peyton
52. Audrey
53. Claire
54. Arianna
55. Julia
56. Aaliyah
57. Kylie
58. Lauren
59. Sophie
60. Sydney
61. Camila
62. Jasmine
63. Morgan
64. Alexandra
65. Jocelyn
66. Gianna
67. Maya
68. Kimberly
69. Mackenzie
70. Katherine
71. Destiny
72. Brooke
73. Trinity
74. Faith
75. Lucy

76. Madelyn
77. Madeline
78. Bailey
79. Payton
80. Andrea
81. Autumn
82. Melanie
83. Ariana
84. Serenity
85. Stella
86. Maria
87. Molly
88. Caroline
89. Genesis
90. Kaitlyn
91. Eva
92. Jessica
93. Angelina
94. Valeria
95. Gabrielle
96. Naomi
97. Mariah
98. Natalia
99. Paige
100. Rachel
101. Mya
102. Rylee

103. Katelyn
104. Ellie
105. Isabelle
106. Vanessa
107. Lilly
108. London
109. Mary
110. Kennedy
111. Lydia
112. Jordyn
113. Ruby
114. Scarlett
115. Jade
116. Isabel
117. Annabelle
118. Sadie
119. Harper
120. Jennifer
121. Sara
122. Nicole
123. Violet
124. Liliana
125. Michelle
126. Stephanie
127. Reagan
128. Jada
129. Adriana

130. Gracie
131. Megan
132. Jayla
133. Kendall
134. Lyla
135. Amy
136. Reese
137. Rebecca
138. Laila
139. Kylee
140. Izabella
141. Jenna
142. Brooklynn
143. Aliyah
144. Piper
145. Juliana
146. Mckenzie
147. Giselle
148. Gabriela
149. Valerie
150. Daniela
151. Daisy
152. Valentina
153. Makenzie
154. Haley
155. Lila
156. Ashlyn

157. Melissa
158. Vivian
159. Nora
160. Angela
161. Katie
162. Hayden
163. Elena
164. Summer
165. Eleanor
166. Keira
167. Clara
168. Jillian
169. Eliana
170. Alana
171. Jacqueline
172. Alice
173. Adrianna
174. Alivia
175. Miranda
176. Julianna
177. Aniyah
178. Jordan
179. Mikayla
180. Eden
181. Skylar
182. Margaret
183. Briana

184. Ryleigh
185. Shelby
186. Josephine
187. Delilah
188. Amanda
189. Allie
190. Addyson
191. Diana
192. Brielle
193. Catherine
194. Angel
195. Danielle
196. Elise
197. Leslie
198. Melody
199. Ana
200. Penelope
201. Makenna
202. Aurora
203. Marissa
204. Leila
205. Alexandria
206. Kendra
207. Alaina
208. Delaney
209. Kate
210. Sienna

211. Lola

212. Jayden

213. Ariel

214. Erin

215. Sierra

216. Hadley

217. Miley

218. Carly

219. Sabrina

220. Alicia

221. Tessa

222. Chelsea

223. Aubree

224. Amber

225. Maggie

226. Amaya

227. Cadence

228. Mckenna

229. Cheyenne

230. Kathryn

231. Kinley

232. Maci

233. Kelsey

234. Marley

235. Alayna

236. Jayda

237. Callie

238. Paisley
239. Ashlynn
240. Eliza
241. Lexi
242. Alexia
243. Teagan
244. Kayleigh
245. Hope
246. Karen
247. Nadia
248. Cassidy
249. Harmony
250. Alondra
251. Jazmin
252. Breanna
253. Quinn
254. Christina
255. Kyla
256. Adalyn
257. Fiona
258. Kaydence
259. Allyson
260. Josie
261. Mariana
262. Hazel
263. Haylee
264. Alina

265. Lucia
266. Danna
267. Esther
268. Leilani
269. Alison
270. Fatima
271. Jazmine
272. Ximena
273. Camille
274. Presley
275. Laura
276. Cora
277. Cecilia
278. Alejandra
279. Genevieve
280. Bianca
281. Camryn
282. Mallory
283. Esmeralda
284. Abby
285. Juliet
286. Brynn
287. Dakota
288. Karina
289. Londyn
290. Willow
291. Kara

292. Macy
293. Maddison
294. Kyleigh
295. Veronica
296. Daniella
297. Isla
298. Norah
299. Ivy
300. Caitlyn
301. Kamryn
302. Malia
303. Heidi
304. Miriam
305. Joanna
306. Kelly
307. Kinsley
308. Kira
309. Phoebe
310. Annabella
311. Tiffany
312. Emery
313. Katelynn
314. Carmen
315. Emerson
316. Iris
317. Emely
318. Crystal

319. Nina
320. Madeleine
321. Rylie
322. Adeline
323. Karla
324. Heaven
325. Kiara
326. Georgia
327. Paris
328. Cassandra
329. Guadalupe
330. Selena
331. Lilah
332. Madilyn
333. Evangeline
334. Tiana
335. Tatum
336. Aniya
337. Rose
338. Madisyn
339. Kaelyn
340. Caitlin
341. Audrina
342. Fernanda
343. Luna
344. Sasha
345. Angelica

346. Jasmin
347. Lilliana
348. Ruth
349. Kyra
350. Emilia
351. Ayla
352. Janiyah
353. Ainsley
354. Courtney
355. Yaretzi
356. Aria
357. Lia
358. Maliyah
359. Raegan
360. Athena
361. Madalyn
362. Tatiana
363. Monica
364. Mila
365. Anastasia
366. Noelle
367. Julissa
368. Jaelyn
369. Bethany
370. Imani
371. Juliette
372. Kenzie

373. Macie
374. Savanna
375. Jamie
376. Giuliana
377. Kiley
378. April
379. Joselyn
380. Cynthia
381. Kailey
382. Lena
383. Alessandra
384. Jane
385. Adelyn
386. Arabella
387. Nayeli
388. Carolina
389. Julie
390. Gia
391. Kaylie
392. Michaela
393. Amiyah
394. Janelle
395. Annie
396. Baylee
397. Elaina
398. Madelynn
399. Kaylin

400. Jimena
401. Lindsey
402. Lyric
403. Addisyn
404. Rebekah
405. Nyla
406. Anya
407. Jazlyn
408. Finley
409. Dulce
410. Melany
411. Itzel
412. Holly
413. Scarlet
414. Talia
415. Cameron
416. Cali
417. Angie
418. Kiera
419. Elle
420. Estrella
421. Elliana
422. Journey
423. Sarai
424. Erica
425. Danica
426. Brenda

427. Brittany
428. Vivienne
429. Erika
430. Hayley
431. Mikaela
432. Kamila
433. Harley
434. Adelaide
435. Brylee
436. Nataly
437. Helen
438. Kadence
439. Kailyn
440. Johanna
441. Lacey
442. Aubrie
443. Ciara
444. Madyson
445. Adalynn
446. Shayla
447. Janiya
448. Bridget
449. Gemma
450. Lilian
451. Paola
452. Jayleen
453. Lillie

454. Serena
455. Aleah
456. Braelyn
457. Celeste
458. Tenley
459. Natasha
460. Kassidy
461. Amari
462. Charlie
463. Brisa
464. Dana
465. Parker
466. Aileen
467. Annika
468. Lexie
469. Nia
470. Brenna
471. Sage
472. Emilee
473. Jaliyah
474. Desiree
475. Anabelle
476. Anahi
477. Skyler
478. Anaya
479. Dayana
480. Kayden

481. Lana
482. Lucille
483. Lilyana
484. Logan
485. Viviana
486. Joy
487. Priscilla
488. Daphne
489. Denise
490. Skye
491. Zariah
492. Kennedi
493. Rowan
494. Francesca
495. Elisa
496. Jaylynn
497. Amira
498. Lizbeth
499. Kimora
500. Kenley
501. Lauryn
502. Melina
503. Gloria
504. Jaelynn
505. Abbigail
506. Arielle
507. Alyson

508. Camilla
509. Brynlee
510. Liberty
511. Myla
512. Alissa
513. Marlee
514. Claudia
515. Hanna
516. Danika
517. Sandra
518. Alanna
519. Hailee
520. Jaycee
521. Nancy
522. Caylee
523. Miracle
524. Gracelyn
525. Annalise
526. Liana
527. Yareli
528. Cindy
529. Marisol
530. Eloise
531. Lorelei
532. Asia
533. Bailee
534. Helena

535. Kali
536. Maeve
537. Jaida
538. Justice
539. Aiyana
540. Kassandra
541. Anika
542. Whitney
543. Laney
544. Natalee
545. Kaia
546. Olive
547. Marilyn
548. Aryanna
549. Farrah
550. Clarissa
551. Halle
552. Ada
553. Amani
554. Janessa
555. Sylvia
556. Mckinley
557. Charlee
558. Aleena
559. Skyla
560. Meghan
561. Madilynn

562. Bristol

563. Giana

564. Rosa

565. Tori

566. Gwendolyn

567. Kaliyah

568. Lea

569. Isabela

570. Shaniya

571. Dylan

572. Averie

573. Aylin

574. Kristen

575. Marie

576. Hallie

577. Kaylynn

578. Zoie

579. Saniyah

580. Lesly

581. Madalynn

582. Kiana

583. Kaleigh

584. Yasmin

585. Wendy

586. Anabella

587. Rihanna

588. Regina

589. Eve
590. Rosalie
591. Elisabeth
592. Kristina
593. Sloane
594. Amya
595. Kathleen
596. Lindsay
597. June
598. Aspen
599. Elsa
600. Nylah
601. Perla
602. Casey
603. Meredith
604. Raquel
605. Siena
606. Samara
607. Saniya
608. Anne
609. Virginia
610. Raven
611. Ayanna
612. Jaylee
613. Jaylin
614. Mckayla
615. Patricia

616. Mariam
617. Sherlyn
618. Lainey
619. Nathalie
620. Shiloh
621. Maia
622. Aimee
623. Isis
624. Linda
625. Jazlynn
626. Raelynn
627. Angelique
628. Annabel
629. Maleah
630. Ryan
631. Paityn
632. Elyse
633. Adelynn
634. Ansley
635. Jadyn
636. Joslyn
637. Kourtney
638. Myah
639. Diamond
640. Marina
641. Bryanna
642. Cara

643. Tabitha
644. Haleigh
645. Selah
646. Elsie
647. Jaylene
648. Leighton
649. Lailah
650. Dahlia
651. Haven
652. Amara
653. Arely
654. Aliya
655. Jaylah
656. Briley
657. Karlee
658. Sariah
659. America
660. Brinley
661. Taryn
662. Amiya
663. Kailee
664. Milan
665. Kaitlin
666. Greta
667. Mercedes
668. Phoenix
669. Lilianna

670. Sidney
671. Alisson
672. Mollie
673. Christine
674. Ellen
675. Vera
676. Taraji
677. Noemi
678. Kallie
679. Keyla
680. Simone
681. Amelie
682. Aisha
683. Catalina
684. Clare
685. Heather
686. Ally
687. Shannon
688. Jessie
689. Taliyah
690. Zion
691. Jordynn
692. Luciana
693. Miah
694. Irene
695. Teresa
696. Adrienne

697. Yesenia
698. Paloma
699. Jaqueline
700. Leanna
701. Rachael
702. Jaiden
703. Janae
704. Jolie
705. Evie
706. Macey
707. Amina
708. Destinee
709. Martha
710. Barbara
711. Abril
712. Deanna
713. Alani
714. Jocelynn
715. Kenya
716. Kaitlynn
717. Sonia
718. Zara
719. Regan
720. Lisa
721. Rosemary
722. Krystal
723. Paulina

724. Elin
725. Evelynn
726. Ali
727. Ariella
728. Alena
729. Corinne
730. Alia
731. Jazmyn
732. Jayde
733. Raelyn
734. Emilie
735. Jakayla
736. Chaya
737. Karissa
738. Laylah
739. Cheyanne
740. Mariyah
741. Carolyn
742. Cecelia
743. Celia
744. Luz
745. Emmalyn
746. Zaniyah
747. Kaiya
748. Leyla
749. Lorelai
750. Iliana

751. Giada
752. Giovanna
753. Cherish
754. Carla
755. Carlee
756. Carley
757. Gisselle
758. Campbell
759. Lylah
760. Adyson
761. Aryana
762. Jaden
763. Larissa
764. Felicity
765. Julianne
766. Tamia
767. Ivanna
768. Natalya
769. Reyna
770. Ingrid
771. Kaya
772. Kaylyn
773. Yoselin
774. Bria
775. Tara
776. Cristina
777. Deborah

778. Harlow
779. Haylie
780. Maryam
781. Carlie
782. Frances
783. Jenny
784. Sawyer
785. Ayana
786. Alisha
787. Sanaa
788. Jaidyn
789. Moriah
790. Rylan
791. Yaritza
792. Susan
793. Allisson
794. Emmalee
795. Kasey
796. Tianna
797. Kaylen
798. Libby
799. Elaine
800. Matilda
801. Patience
802. Analia
803. Sharon
804. Nathaly

805. Aliana

806. Karlie

807. Maritza

808. Yazmin

809. Heidy

810. Tess

811. Karsyn

812. Emelia

813. Chanel

814. Armani

815. Marisa

816. Chana

817. Paula

818. Azul

819. Alyvia

820. Edith

821. Abbie

822. Araceli

823. Aliza

824. Amirah

825. Ember

826. Livia

827. Zaria

828. Isabell

829. Carissa

830. Avah

831. Hayleigh

832. Leia

833. Akira

834. Beatrice

835. Cailyn

836. Charley

837. Eileen

838. Ireland

839. Kenna

840. Kiersten

841. Hadassah

842. Demi

843. Gracelynn

844. Hana

845. Kirsten

846. Malaya

847. Micah

848. Lina

849. Alayah

850. Alma

851. Lillianna

852. Angeline

853. Ayleen

854. Kelsie

855. Charity

856. Mira

857. Jemma

858. Ashlee

859. Nola
860. Raina
861. Jacquelyn
862. Jaylyn
863. Lilyanna
864. Mayra
865. Belinda
866. Bree
867. Katrina
868. Millie
869. Belen
870. Mara
871. Renee
872. Zariyah
873. Rubi
874. Joyce
875. Ryann
876. Lilia
877. Shyla
878. Kyndall
879. Judith
880. Kendal
881. Lara
882. Meadow
883. Salma
884. Tania
885. Elianna

886. Kynlee
887. Abbey
888. Neveah
889. Rayne
890. Sarahi
891. Briella
892. Stacy
893. Braelynn
894. Janet
895. Laniyah
896. Saige
897. Karma
898. Lizeth
899. Rayna
900. Makena
901. Princess
902. Marlene
903. Riya
904. Dominique
905. Azaria
906. Jaylen
907. Kaelynn
908. Adele
909. Britney
910. Karly
911. Ann
912. Abigale

913. Caydence
914. Janiah
915. Adelina
916. Charli
917. Emersyn
918. Diya
919. Kayleen
920. Marianna
921. Esme
922. Maliah
923. Abagail
924. Alisa
925. Carleigh
926. Dixie
927. Nathalia
928. Karli
929. Shyanne
930. Yamilet
931. Payten
932. Roselyn
933. Jewel
934. Journee
935. Mattie
936. Aiyanna
937. Arya
938. Damaris
939. Tegan

940. Theresa
941. Yamileth
942. Emmy
943. Averi
944. Mylee
945. Kylah
946. Anabel
947. Thalia
948. Carina
949. Esperanza
950. Jamya
951. Kierra
952. Sydnee
953. Audriana
954. Shania
955. Ivana
956. Micaela
957. Kinsey
958. Azariah
959. Kai
960. Precious
961. Kimber
962. Mina
963. Pearl
964. Alannah
965. Kloe
966. Lorena

967. Myra
968. Willa
969. Dalia
970. Jolene
971. Kairi
972. River
973. Shaylee
974. Addilyn
975. Alexus
976. Jaslene
977. India
978. Milagros
979. Reina
980. Zuri
981. Evelin
982. Stephany
983. Ariah
984. Donna
985. Pamela
986. Amiah
987. Devyn
988. Mae
989. Xiomara
990. Aracely
991. Bryleigh
992. Lilith
993. Leona

994. Aleigha
995. Savanah
996. Alaysia
997. Leilah
998. Violeta
999. Charleigh
1000. Dania

# Chapter 4:
# Famous Baby Names

Celebrities often pick very unique names for their children. Some people love this, others hate it, while some just find it funny!

Either way, here's a list of some extremely unique names that celebrities have chosen for their children. Use it as inspiration, or just for a laugh – up to you!

| | |
|---|---|
| Alanis Morissette and Mario 'Souleye' Treadway (Singer and Musician) | Ever Imre (son) |
| Alec Baldwin and Kim Basinger (Actor and Actress) | Ireland (daughter) |
| Alice Cooper (Musician) | Sonora Rosc (daughter)<br><br>Calico Dashiell (son) |
| Alicia Keys and Swizz Beats (Singer and Producer) | Egypt Daoud (son) |
| Alicia Silverstone (Actress) | Bear Blu (son) |
| Amy Adams (Actress) | Aviana Olea (daughter) |

| Ashlee Simpson and Pete Wentz (Singer and Musician) | Bronx Mowgli (son) |
| Barbara Hershey and David Carradine (Actress and Actor) | Free (son) |
| Ben Affleck and Jennifer Garner (Actor and Actress) | Violet Anne (daughter)<br><br>Seraphina Rose Elizabeth (daughter) |
| Benjamin Bratt (Actor) | Mateo Braverly (son) |
| Beyoncé Knowles and Jay-Z (Singer and Rapper) | Blue Ivy (daughter) |
| Bob Geldof and Paula Yates (Musician and TV Host) | Fifi Trixibelle (daughter)<br><br>Peaches Honeyblossom (daughter)<br><br>Little Pixie (daughter) |
| Bono (Musician) | Memphis Eve (daughter) |
| Brad Pitt and Angelina Jolie (Actor and Actress) | Zahara Marley (daughter)<br><br>Maddox Chivan Thomton (son) |

Pax Thien (son)

Shiloh Nouvel (daughter)

Knox Leon (twin son)

Vivienne Marcheline (twin daughter)

| | |
|---|---|
| Brooke Burke (TV Personality) | Neriah Shae (daughter) |
| | Sierra Sky (daughter) |
| | Heaven Rain (daughter) |
| | Shaya Braven (daughter) |
| Brooke Shields (Actress) | Grier Hammond (daughter) |
| | Rowan Francis (daughter) |
| Bruce Willis and Demi Moore (Actor and Actress) | Rumer Glen (daughter) |
| | Scout Larue (daughter) |
| | Tallulah Belle (daughter) |
| Bryan Adams (Singer) | Mirabella Bunny (daughter) |
| Casey Affleck and Summer Phoenix (Actor and Actress) | Indiana August (son) |

| | |
|---|---|
| Casey Kasem (Radio Host) | Liberty (daughter) |
| Cher (Musician) | Chastity (daughter) |
| | Elijah Blue (son) |
| Chris Rock (Comedian/Actor) | Lola Simone (daughter) |
| | Zahra Savannah (daughter) |
| Christie Brinkley (Model) | Sailor Lee (daughter) |
| Clint Eastwood (Actor) | Francesca (daughter) |
| | Kimber (daughter) |
| Courteney Cox and David Arquette (Actress and Actor) | Coco Riley (daughter) |
| Daniel Baldwin (Actor) | Atticus (son) |
| Daniel Day Lewis (Actor) | Cashel Blake (son) |
| | Ronan Cal (son) |
| David Duchovny and Tea Leoni (Actor and Actress) | Madeline West (daughter) |
| | Kyd Miller (son) |

| David and Victoria Beckham (Athlete and Singer) | Brooklyn Joseph (son) |
| | Romeo James (son) |
| | Cruz David (son) |
| | Harper Seven (daughter) |
| David Bowie (Musician) | Duncan Zowie Heywood Jones (son) |
| Debra Messing (Actress) | Roman Zelman (son) |
| Drea de Matteo and Shooter Jennings (Actress and Musician) | Alabama Gypsyrose (daughter) |
| | Waylon Albert 'Blackjack' (son) |
| Eddie Murphy (Comedian/Actor) | Zola Ivy (daughter) |
| Elle MacPherson (Model) | Arpad Flynn Alexander (son) |
| | Aurelius Cy Andrea (daughter) |
| Elton John (Musician) and David Furnish | Zachary Jackson Levon (son) |

Emma Thompson (Actress) — Gaia Romilly (daughter)

Erykah Badu (Musician) — Seven Sirius (son)

Puma (daughter)

Forest Whitaker (Actor) — Ocean Alexander (son)

Sonnet Noel (daughter)

True Isabella Summer (daughter)

Frank Zappa (Musician) — Diva Muffin (daughter)

Moon Unit (daughter)

Ian Donald Calvin Euclid "Dweezil" (son)

Ahmet Rodan (son)

Gary Oldman (Actor) — Gulliver Flynn (son)

Alfie (son)

Gillian Anderson (Actress) — Piper Maru (daughter)

Gwen Stefani and Gavin Rossdale (Singer and Musician) — Kingston James McGregor (son)

Zuma Nesta Rock (son)

| | |
|---|---|
| Gywneth Paltrow and Chris Martin (Actress and Musician) | Apple Blythe Alison (daughter)<br><br>Moses (son) |
| Heidi Klum and Seal (Model and Singer) | Helene "Leni" (daughter)<br><br>Henry Gunther Ademola Dashtu (son)<br><br>Johan Riley Fyodor Taiwo (son)<br><br>Lou Sulola (daughter) |
| Heath Ledger and Michelle Williams (Actor and Actress) | Matilda Rose (daughter) |
| Helen Hunt (Actress) | Makena'lei Gordon (daughter) |
| Isla Fisher and Sacha Baron Cohen (Actress and Comedian) | Olive (daughter)<br><br>Elula (daughter) |
| Jamie Oliver and Juliette Norton (Chef and Model) | Poppy Honey (daughter)<br><br>Daisy Boo (daughter)<br><br>Petal Blossom Rainbow |

(daughter)

Buddy Bear Maurice (son)

January Jones (Actress) — Xander Dane (son)

Jason Bateman (Actor) — Francesca Nora (daughter)

Maple Sylvie (daughter)

Jason Lee (Actor) — Pilot Inspektor (son)

Casper (daughter)

Jason Schwartzman (Actor) — Marlowe Rivers (daughter)

Jenna Fischer (Actress) — Weston Lee (son)

Jennifer Connelly and Paul Bettany (Actress and Actor) — Kai (son from Jennifer's previous relationship)

Stellan (son)

Agnes Lark (daughter)

Jerry Seinfeld (Comedian) — Sascha (daughter)

Julien Kal (son)

Shepherd Kellen (son)

| | |
|---|---|
| Jessica Alba and Cash Warren (Actress and Producer) | Honor Marie (daughter)<br><br>Haven Garner (daughter) |
| John Cougar Mellencamp (Musician) | Hud (son)<br><br>Spec Wildhorse (son) |
| Julia Roberts (Actress) | Hazel Patricia (twin daughter)<br><br>Phinnaeus Walter (twin son) |
| Kate Hudson (Actress) | Ryder Russell (son with musician Chris Robinson)<br><br>Bingham Hawn (son with musician Matthew Bellamy) |
| Kimberley Williams and Brad Paisley (Actress and Musician) | William Huckleberry (son) |
| Kyra Sedgwick and Kevin Bacon (Actress and Actor) | Sosie Ruth (daughter)<br><br>Travis Sedg (son) |
| Larry King (TV host) | Chance Armstrong (son)<br><br>Cannon Edward (son) |

| Marcia Cross (Actress) | Eden (twin daughter) |
| | Savannah (twin daughter) |
| Mariah Carey and Nick Cannon (Singer and Actor) | Monroe (twin daughter) |
| | Moroccan "Roc" Scott (twin son) |
| Matt Lauer (TV host) | Thijs (son) |
| Mike Myers (Comedian) | Spike (son) |
| Mike Tyson (Boxer) | Mikey (son) |
| | D'Amato (son) |
| | Rayna (daughter) |
| | Amir (son) |
| | Miguel (son) |
| | Exodus (daughter) |
| | Milan (daughter) |
| | Morocco (son) |
| Natalie Portman (Actress) | Aleph (son) |
| Neil Patrick Harris and | Gideon Scott (twin son) |

| David Burtka (Actors) | Harper Grace (twin daughter) |
| Nicholas Cage (Actor) | Kal El Coppola (son) |
| Nick Nolte (Actor) | Brawley King (son) |
| Nicole Kidman and Keith Urban (Actress and Musician) | Sunday Rose (daughter)<br>Faith Margaret (daughter) |
| Nicole Richie and Joel Madden (Socialite and Musician) | Harlow Winter Kate (daughter)<br>Sparrow James Midnight (son) |
| Patricia Arquette (Actress) | Enzo Rossi (son) |
| Paul Anderson and Milla Jovovich (Director and Actress) | Ever Gabo (daughter) |
| Penn Jillette (Entertainer) | Moxie CrimeFighter (daughter)<br>Zolten (son) |
| Phylicia and Ahmad Rashad (Actress and Sports | Condola Phylea (daughter) |

Announcer)

Richard Gere (Actor) — Homer James Jigme (son)

Robert Rodriguez (Director) — Rocket Valentin (son)

Racer Maximilliano (son)

Rebel Antonio (son)

Rogue (son)

Rhiannon (daughter)

Russell Crowe (Actor) — Tennyson (son)

Steve Buscemi (Actor) — Lucien (son)

Sean Combs (Musician) — Jessie James (twin daughter)

D'Lila Star (twin daughter)

Selma Blair (Actress) — Arthur Saint (son)

Stephen Spielberg and Kate Capshaw (Director and Actress) — Jessica (daughter)

Max Samuel (son)

Theo (son)

Sasha Rebecca (daughter)

Sawyer Avery (son)

Mikaela George (daughter)

Destry Allyn (daughter)

Sting (Musician)

Joseph (son)

Fuchsia Catherine (daughter)

Bridget Michael "Micky" (daughter)

Jake (son)

Eliot Pauline "Coco" (daughter)

Giacomo Luke (son)

Sylvester Stallone (Actor)

Sage Moonblood (daughter)

Seargeoh (son)

Sophia Rose (daughter)

Sistine Rose (daughter)

Scarlet Rose (daughter)

Taboo (Musician)

Journey Jameson (son)

| Tina Fey (Actress) | Alice Zenobia (daughter) |
| | Penelope Athena (daughter) |
| Tobey Maguire (Actor) | Ruby Sweetheart (daughter) |
| | Otis Tobias (son) |
| Tom Cruise and Katie Holmes (Actor and Actress) | Suri (daughter) |
| Toni Collette (Actress) | Sage (daughter) |
| | Arlo (son) |
| Uma Thurman and Ethan Hawke (Actress and Actor) | Levon Green (son) |
| Usher Raymond IV (Singer) | Usher Raymond V (son) |
| | Naviyd Ely (son) |
| Will and Jada Pinkett Smith (Actor and Actress) | Jaden Christopher Syre (son) |
| | Willow Camille Reign (daughter) |

Woody Allen and Mia Farrow
(Actor/Director and Actress)

Satchel Seamus (son)

Moses Amadeus (son)

95

# Chapter 5:
# Unique Names

Some people love unique names that have a bit of meaning to them, and stand out from the crowd!

This chapter includes a range of unique names for both boys and girls for your perusal. Enjoy!

## Names from locations

Many people like to name their children after locations. This trend is getting a lot more popular, especially with celebrities!

Most of these names can be unisex, as they don't have any connection anything other than a location!

- Clyde – a river in Scotland
- Fraser – Town in France
- Jordan – country in the Middle East
- Paris – capital of France
- Maine – one of the 50 states in the US
- France – a country in Western Europe
- Kailash – a Himalayan mountain
- Acton – town in Britain
- Louvain – city in Belgium
- Sidney – City in Australia
- Kerry – county in Ireland
- Daryl – area in France
- Nevada – western US state

## Names of Historical References

Naming your child after a historic event or place in time gives your child's name quite a unique meaning. Below are some great examples you might like to consider.

Machias

Sturbridge

Montpelier

Lexington

Walden

Concord

Parker

## Names from the Bible

Biblical names are always popular. Pick from the lists below!

### Boy's Names

Andrew – Disciple of Jesus

Like – Apostle

Stephen – a martyr

Jason – colleague of Paul

Joseph – father of Jesus

Jairus – leader of the synagogue

Alexander – son of the man who carried Jesus' cross

James – brother of Jesus

Timothy – disciple of Paul

**Girl's Names**

Anna – a prophetess

Julia – woman greeted by the apostle Paul

Mary – Mother of Jesus

Bethany – a village in the book of Luke

Eunice – mother of Timothy

Magdala – town of Mary Magdalene

Hoebe – woman in the book of Romans

Salome – mother of John the Apostle

**Names of Angels**

Gabriel – guardian angel of fire

Michael – guardian angel of the threshold

Tubiel – guardian angel of summer

Zadkiel – guardian angel of benevolence

Attarib – guardian angel of winter

## Cultural Tradition Names

You might want to consider some names from different cultures. These are certainly unique!

## Scandinavian Names

**Boy's Names**

Anders

Bjørn

Gustaf

Per

Karl

Dag

Oskar

Rolf

Jens

Olaf

Lars

Nil

## Girl's Names

Astrid

Britta

Dagmar

Eva

Grete

Ingrid

Siane

Ulta

Kari

Anna

Heide

Margareta

Elisabeth

# Native American Names

## Boy's Names

Chaska – first son

Len – meaning flute

Pezi – grass

Galegina – male deer

Nashoba – wolf

Diwali - bowl

Hohots – bear

Sani – old

Zotom – one who bites

## Girl's Names

Chapa – Beaver

Kaya – older sister

Opa – owl

Sahkyo – mink

Inola – black fox

Taima – fox

Natane – daughter

Acadia – village

Eyota – great

Zitkala – bird

<u>**Hindu Names**</u>

**Boy's Names**

Amar

Anand

Kala

Kesin

Pramod

Vadin

Krishna

Adri

Balin

Valin

Vasin

Vinod

Rohin

Hardeep

Dalal

**Girl's Names**

Anala

Deva

Chandi

Kalinda

Lalita

Natesa

Rudra

Sita

Veda

## **<u>Greek Mythological Figures</u>**

Greek mythology is filled with interesting names that not only sound great, they also have meaning and great stories behind them! Check out some of the best mythological names below.

## **Male Gods - Inspirational Names for Boys**

Adonis – God of beauty

Res – God of war

Orion – God of the hunt

Pan – God of the shepherds

Triton – God of the sea

Apollo – God of war

Eros – God of love

Hermes – Messenger of the gods

Pontus – God of the sea

Zeus – King of the gods

Atlas – held the world on his shoulders

Helios – God of the sun

## **Female Gods - Inspirational Names for Girls**

Artemis – Goddess of nature

Athena – Goddess of wisdom

Eris – Goddess of debate

Aphrodite – Goddess of beauty

Hestia – Goddess of the home

Nike – Goddess of victory

Selena – Goddess of the moon

Persephone – goddess of the spring and rebirth

Iris – Goddess of the rainbow

Demeter – Goddess of the Earth

## Roman Mythological Names

Roman mythology, just like Greek, includes some really interesting names with stories behind them!

## Inspirational Names for Boys

Hercules – Jove's son

Sol – God of the sun

Mars – God of war

Romulus – founder of Rome

Jupiter – God of all

Cupid – God of love

Janus – God of doorways

Mercury – messenger of the gods

Saturn – God of harvests

Ulysses – King of Ithaca

Vulcan – God of fire

## Inspirational Names for Girls

Ceres – Goddess of farming

Diana – Goddess of the moon

Luna – Goddess of the moon

Pomona – Goddess of fruit tress

Vesta – Goddess of the home

Aurora- Goddess of the sunrise

Minerva – Goddess of wisdom

Terra – Goddess of the earth

Victoria – Goddess of Victory

Flora- Goddess of the flowers

Latona – Mother of Dianna and Apollo

# Conclusion

Thanks again for taking the time to use this book!

By now you've seen literally thousands of different baby names! I hope that one has caught your attention, and that you've now settled on the perfect name! Once again, congratulations, and I wish you the very best of luck in parenthood!

If you enjoyed this book, please take the time to leave me a review on Amazon. I really appreciate your honest feedback, and it helps me to continue producing high quality books.